The Power of Positive Mindset Motivational Strategies for Student Achievement

Quentin

Copyright © [2023]

Author: Quentin

Title: The Power of Positive Mindset Motivational Strategies for Student Achievement

This book is a product of [Publisher's Quentin]

ISBN:

TABLE OF CONTENTS

Chapter 1: The Power of a Positive Mindset

Understanding the Mindset

In the realm of educational psychology, the concept of mindset has gained significant attention in recent years. The way we perceive ourselves, our abilities, and our potential has a profound impact on our academic achievements. Developing a positive mindset is crucial for success in any academic endeavor. In this subchapter, we will delve into the depths of understanding the mindset and explore how it can be harnessed to unlock our true potential.

To comprehend the mindset, we must first recognize the two main types: the fixed mindset and the growth mindset. A fixed mindset is characterized by the belief that our abilities and intelligence are fixed traits, incapable of improvement. On the other hand, a growth mindset thrives on the notion that our skills and intelligence can be developed through dedication, hard work, and perseverance.

It is imperative to understand that our mindset is not innate, but rather a product of our upbringing, experiences, and environment. By becoming aware of our mindset and its impact on our academic journey, we can actively work towards cultivating a growth mindset.

One of the key elements in developing a growth mindset is embracing challenges. Instead of fearing failure or setbacks, we should view challenges as opportunities for growth and learning. By reframing our perception of obstacles, we can approach them with resilience and determination, knowing that even if we stumble, it is an integral part of the learning process.

Another essential aspect of the growth mindset is the power of yet. Instead of saying "I can't do this," adding the word yet at the end transforms it into "I can't do this yet." This small shift in language signifies that we are on a journey of continuous improvement and that our current limitations do not define our future capabilities.

Furthermore, adopting a growth mindset involves embracing the power of positive self-talk. Our inner dialogue significantly influences our beliefs and actions. By replacing self-doubt and self-criticism with affirmations and encouragement, we can cultivate a positive mindset that propels us towards success.

Understanding the mindset is not a one-time endeavor. It requires consistent effort, self-reflection, and a willingness to challenge our existing beliefs and assumptions. By developing a growth mindset, we can unlock our true potential, overcome obstacles, and achieve academic excellence.

In conclusion, understanding the mindset is a crucial step towards achieving success as a student. By recognizing the difference between a fixed mindset and a growth mindset, we can actively work towards cultivating a positive mindset that propels us towards academic achievement. Embracing challenges, adopting the power of yet, and practicing positive self-talk are essential strategies in developing a growth mindset. Remember, your mindset is not fixed, but malleable. With the right mindset, you can conquer any academic challenge and unlock your true potential.

The Impact of Mindset on Student Achievement

Introduction:
In the realm of educational psychology, one concept reigns supreme - mindset. Your mindset, or the way you think about your abilities and potential, has a profound impact on your academic achievements. In this subchapter, we will explore the powerful influence of mindset on student achievement and delve into strategies that can help you develop a positive mindset for academic success.

Understanding   Mindset:
Mindset refers to your beliefs about your intelligence, abilities, and potential to learn and grow. There are two primary mindsets: fixed mindset and growth mindset. A fixed mindset assumes that intelligence and abilities are fixed traits, while a growth mindset believes that intelligence and abilities can be developed through effort, learning, and perseverance.

The   Power   of   a   Growth   Mindset:
Research has consistently shown that students with a growth mindset outperform those with a fixed mindset. Embracing a growth mindset opens doors to new possibilities, fuels motivation, and enhances academic achievements. With a growth mindset, setbacks are seen as opportunities for learning and growth, rather than as indicators of failure.

Cultivating   a   Growth   Mindset:
Developing a growth mindset requires intentional effort and practice. Start by recognizing and challenging your own fixed mindset beliefs. Replace statements like "I'm just not good at math" with "I can improve my math skills with practice and effort." Set realistic goals and focus on the process of learning rather than just the outcomes.

Embrace challenges as opportunities to grow, seek feedback as a chance to improve, and look to successful role models who demonstrate a growth mindset.

Overcoming Obstacles:
Obstacles are inevitable on the path to success, but with a growth mindset, they become stepping stones rather than roadblocks. Embrace a positive attitude towards challenges, and approach them with determination and resilience. Learn from failures, adjust strategies, and persevere. Remember that intelligence and abilities can be developed with effort and dedication.

Conclusion:
In conclusion, your mindset holds the key to unlocking your academic potential. By adopting a growth mindset and cultivating positive beliefs about your abilities, you can overcome obstacles, embrace challenges, and achieve remarkable success in your educational journey. Embrace the power of a growth mindset and witness the transformative impact it can have on your student achievement.

Chapter 2: Developing a Positive Mindset

Identifying and Overcoming Negative Self-Talk

In the journey towards achieving success and personal growth, one of the biggest hurdles that students often face is negative self-talk. Negative self-talk refers to the internal dialogue or thoughts that undermine our confidence, self-esteem, and ability to reach our full potential. It is a detrimental habit that can hinder our progress and prevent us from achieving our goals. However, by understanding and overcoming negative self-talk, students can unlock their true potential and pave the way for success.

The first step in addressing negative self-talk is to become aware of it. Often, negative self-talk operates on autopilot, and we may not even realize the impact it has on our thoughts and actions. Paying attention to our inner dialogue and recognizing negative patterns is crucial. It could be thoughts like "I'm not smart enough" or "I always mess things up." By identifying these negative thoughts, we can challenge them and replace them with positive affirmations.

Educational psychology teaches us that positive self-talk plays a vital role in shaping our mindset and behavior. By replacing negative self-talk with positive affirmations, students can rewire their thinking patterns and boost their confidence. For example, instead of saying, "I'm not good at math," students can reframe it as "I am improving my math skills every day." This shift in mindset can have a powerful impact on their motivation and ultimately their achievement.

Furthermore, it is essential to question the validity and reality of our negative self-talk. Often, these thoughts are based on irrational beliefs or past experiences that no longer hold true. By challenging these thoughts and seeking evidence to the contrary, students can gain a more realistic perspective and overcome self-doubt.

Another effective strategy to overcome negative self-talk is to surround oneself with positive influences. By seeking support from friends, family, or mentors who uplift and encourage, students can create an environment that fosters positive self-talk. Moreover, engaging in activities that promote self-reflection, such as journaling or meditation, can help students become more aware of their thoughts and emotions, enabling them to address negative self-talk more effectively.

In conclusion, negative self-talk can be a significant barrier to student achievement. However, by identifying and overcoming this detrimental habit, students can cultivate a positive mindset and reach their full potential. Through awareness, positive affirmations, challenging irrational beliefs, seeking support, and engaging in self-reflection, students can transform their negative self-talk into a powerful tool for personal growth and success. Remember, the power to change lies within you!

Cultivating Self-Confidence

Subchapter: Cultivating Self-Confidence

Introduction:

In the pursuit of academic success, one of the most valuable qualities a student can possess is self-confidence. It acts as a driving force, propelling students towards their goals, and enables them to overcome obstacles with resilience and determination. Cultivating self-confidence is not an innate ability; rather, it is a skill that can be developed through practice and a positive mindset. In this subchapter, we will explore the various strategies and techniques that can help students cultivate self-confidence, leading them to achieve their full potential.

1. Understanding the Power of Self-Belief: Self-confidence starts with believing in oneself. It is crucial for students to recognize their unique abilities, talents, and potential. By acknowledging their strengths and accepting their weaknesses, students can develop a realistic and positive self-image, laying the foundation for self-confidence.

2. Setting Realistic Goals: Goal setting is an essential aspect of cultivating self-confidence. It is important for students to set realistic and achievable goals that align with their interests and abilities. By breaking down larger goals into smaller, manageable tasks, students can experience a sense of accomplishment, boosting their self-confidence along the way.

3. Embracing Failure as a Stepping Stone: Failure is a natural part of the learning process. Rather than viewing failure as a setback, students should embrace it as an opportunity for

growth. By reframing failures as learning experiences, students can develop resilience, perseverance, and a stronger sense of self-confidence.

4.   Visualizing   Success:
Visualization is a powerful technique that can help students build self-confidence. By vividly imagining themselves successfully achieving their goals, students can enhance their belief in their abilities. Visualization techniques, such as creating vision boards or using guided imagery exercises, can boost self-confidence and motivation.

5.   Surrounding   Yourself   with   Positive   Influences:
The company we keep greatly influences our self-confidence. Students should surround themselves with supportive and positive individuals who believe in their abilities. By establishing a network of friends, mentors, and teachers who provide encouragement and constructive feedback, students can reinforce their self-belief and confidence.

6.   Celebrating   Achievements:
Recognizing and celebrating achievements, no matter how small, is vital for cultivating self-confidence. Students should acknowledge their progress and give themselves credit for their accomplishments. By celebrating achievements, students reinforce their belief in their abilities and gain the motivation to continue striving for excellence.

Conclusion:
Cultivating self-confidence is a transformative journey that requires self-awareness, perseverance, and a positive mindset. By understanding the power of self-belief, setting realistic goals, embracing failure, visualizing success, surrounding oneself with positive influences, and celebrating achievements, students can unlock their full potential and achieve remarkable success in their educational

journey. Remember, self-confidence is not a destination but a lifelong skill that can be nurtured and developed, leading to a brighter and more fulfilling future.

Setting Realistic Goals

In the pursuit of success, setting realistic goals is an essential component of achieving our dreams. As students, it is crucial to understand the significance of setting goals that are attainable, measurable, and relevant to our educational journey. By adopting this mindset, we can harness the power of positive thinking and motivate ourselves to excel in our studies.

When it comes to setting realistic goals, it is important to consider our current abilities, resources, and limitations. Unrealistic goals can lead to disappointment and frustration, which may hinder our progress. Instead, we should focus on setting goals that challenge us but are within our reach. For example, if we struggle with time management, it would be unrealistic to expect ourselves to complete all assignments and study for exams in a single day. By breaking down our tasks into smaller, more manageable goals, we can ensure a higher probability of success.

Moreover, setting measurable goals allows us to track our progress and evaluate our efforts. Measurable goals are specific and quantifiable, enabling us to determine if we are moving in the right direction. For instance, instead of setting a vague goal like "improve my grades," we can set a measurable goal such as "achieve a B+ average in all my subjects this semester." This way, we can assess our progress regularly and make adjustments if needed.

Furthermore, setting goals that are relevant to our educational journey is crucial for maintaining motivation and focus. Our goals should align with our long-term aspirations and reflect our personal values. For instance, if we aspire to pursue a career in medicine, setting goals related to maintaining a high GPA and engaging in extracurricular activities that enhance our understanding of the medical field would be relevant and beneficial.

In conclusion, setting realistic goals is a fundamental aspect of achieving success as students. By considering our abilities, resources, and limitations, setting measurable goals, and ensuring their relevance to our educational journey, we can create a positive mindset that propels us towards our desired achievements. Through goal setting, we can overcome challenges, stay motivated, and experience the satisfaction of accomplishing our dreams. So, let us embrace the power of setting realistic goals and unlock our full potential as students.

Chapter 3: Strategies for Building Motivation

Finding Your Why: Discovering Your Purpose

In the journey of life, it is essential to have a clear sense of purpose – a reason why you wake up every morning and strive to achieve your goals. This subchapter, "Finding Your Why: Discovering Your Purpose," delves into the importance of uncovering your true purpose and how it can positively impact your educational journey. Whether you are a high school student, a college student, or pursuing further studies, understanding your purpose will provide you with the motivation and direction needed for success.

Educational psychology teaches us that individuals who have a strong sense of purpose are more likely to excel academically. When you have a clear purpose, it becomes easier to set meaningful goals and work towards them with determination. Without a purpose, you may find yourself drifting aimlessly, lacking the drive to make the most of your educational opportunities.

So, how can you find your why and discover your purpose? Start by reflecting on your passions and interests. What subjects or activities bring you joy and fulfillment? What do you envision yourself doing in the future? By exploring these questions, you can gain valuable insights into what truly drives you and excites you.

It is also essential to consider the impact you want to make on the world. What positive change do you want to bring about in your community, society, or even globally? When you align your purpose with making a difference, your motivation becomes fueled by a deep sense of responsibility and a desire to contribute positively to the world.

Additionally, don't be afraid to seek guidance from mentors, teachers, and professionals in your field of interest. They can provide valuable insights and help you uncover your true purpose. Engage in conversations, attend workshops, and explore different career paths to gain a broader perspective.

Once you have discovered your purpose, embrace it wholeheartedly. Use it as a guiding force in making decisions, setting goals, and selecting the educational path that aligns with your passion and purpose. Remember, your purpose may evolve and change over time, and that is perfectly normal. The key is to remain open to new possibilities and continue to nurture your growth.

In conclusion, finding your why and discovering your purpose is essential for students pursuing educational success. By aligning your goals with your passions and making a positive impact on the world, you will find the motivation and direction needed to thrive academically. Embrace the process of self-discovery, seek guidance when needed, and let your purpose guide you towards a fulfilling and successful educational journey.

Creating a Vision Board for Success

In the realm of educational psychology, the power of visualization and goal-setting cannot be underestimated. As students, you have immense potential to achieve great things, but it is essential to have a clear vision of what success looks like for you. One effective tool to help you define and manifest your aspirations is a vision board.

A vision board is a visual representation of your goals, dreams, and desires. It serves as a tangible reminder of what you aim to accomplish, providing clarity and motivation along your educational journey. By creating a vision board, you can tap into the power of positive mindset and enhance your chances of achieving academic success.

To begin, gather materials such as a corkboard, poster board, or even a digital platform like Pinterest. Next, reflect on your goals and aspirations. What do you want to achieve in your academic life? Are there specific grades you aim to attain, scholarships you wish to earn, or subjects you want to excel in? Take the time to visualize your ideal future and be specific about what you want to accomplish.

Once you have a clear understanding of your goals, start collecting images, quotes, and affirmations that resonate with your vision. For instance, if you aspire to become a doctor, you could include pictures of medical professionals, stethoscopes, or hospitals. Additionally, find inspirational quotes that motivate you and affirmations that reinforce your belief in your abilities.

Arrange these elements on your vision board in a way that is visually appealing to you. You can create different sections or themes that represent different areas of your academic life, such as study habits, extracurricular activities, or personal growth. Be creative and personalize it to reflect your unique aspirations.

Once your vision board is complete, display it in a prominent place where you can see it daily. Take a few moments each day to visualize yourself achieving your goals and believe in your ability to make them a reality. The visualization process will help train your mind to focus on your objectives and attract opportunities that align with your desires.

Remember, a vision board is not a magical solution that guarantees success overnight. It is a tool to guide and inspire you along your educational journey. Embrace the power of positive mindset, work diligently towards your goals, and use your vision board as a visual reminder of the success you are striving for.

In conclusion, by creating a vision board for success, you are taking a proactive step in shaping your educational path. This powerful tool, rooted in the principles of educational psychology, will help you stay focused, motivated, and determined to achieve your goals. So unleash your creativity, visualize your dreams, and watch as your academic aspirations come to life.

Harnessing the Power of Visualization

Visualization is a powerful technique that can greatly enhance student achievement and success. By harnessing the power of visualization, students can tap into their inner potential and achieve their goals. This subchapter explores the benefits of visualization, how it works, and practical strategies for incorporating visualization into your educational journey.

Research in educational psychology has shown that visualization can have a significant impact on academic performance. When students visualize themselves successfully completing a task or achieving a goal, they are more likely to take the necessary steps to make it happen. This is because visualization activates the same neural pathways in the brain as actually performing the task, reinforcing the belief that success is possible.

The process of visualization involves creating a mental image of what you want to achieve and engaging all your senses to make it as vivid as possible. For example, if you want to excel in a math exam, visualize yourself confidently solving complex problems, feeling the excitement of success, and hearing the applause of your peers. By repeatedly visualizing this scenario, you are programming your mind for success.

To harness the power of visualization, begin by setting clear, specific goals. Whether it's improving your grades, mastering a new skill, or accomplishing a personal milestone, clearly define what you want to achieve. Once you have identified your goals, close your eyes and imagine yourself already achieving them. See yourself studying diligently, participating actively in class, and effortlessly acing exams. Feel the sense of accomplishment and pride that comes with reaching your goals.

Incorporating visualization into your daily routine is essential for its effectiveness. Set aside a few minutes each day to visualize your goals and reinforce positive thoughts. By consistently practicing visualization, you will develop a positive mindset that will drive you towards success.

Additionally, visualization can be combined with other study strategies such as creating vision boards, using affirmations, and practicing mindfulness. By utilizing these techniques together, you can create a powerful synergy that further strengthens your motivation and focus.

In conclusion, harnessing the power of visualization is an invaluable strategy for student achievement. By visualizing success, setting clear goals, and consistently practicing visualization, students can unlock their full potential and achieve remarkable results. Remember, your mind is a powerful tool, and by using visualization techniques, you can shape your reality and create the future you desire.

Chapter 4: Overcoming Obstacles and Challenges

Embracing Failure as a Learning Opportunity

In the journey of academic and personal growth, failure is often regarded as a setback, a sign of weakness or incompetence. However, in the realm of educational psychology, it is increasingly recognized that failure can be a powerful catalyst for growth and success. By reframing failure as a learning opportunity, students can harness its potential to develop resilience, adaptability, and a positive mindset.

One of the key tenets of embracing failure is understanding that mistakes are an integral part of the learning process. As students, we often strive for perfection, fearing the consequences of making errors. However, educational psychologists argue that mistakes provide invaluable insight into our areas of weakness and offer opportunities for improvement. By shifting our perspective and viewing failure as a feedback mechanism, we can identify areas that require further attention and refine our skills accordingly.

Moreover, embracing failure encourages a growth mindset, a belief system that fosters the belief in our ability to develop and grow through effort and perseverance. Educational psychologists emphasize that intelligence and abilities are not fixed traits, but rather can be developed over time with the right mindset. By embracing failure as a stepping stone to improvement, students can cultivate a growth mindset that empowers them to face challenges with determination and resilience.

In addition, failure allows us to develop problem-solving skills and resilience in the face of adversity. When we encounter obstacles and setbacks, we are forced to think creatively and develop alternative strategies. This process enhances our critical thinking abilities and equips us with the necessary skills to navigate future challenges.

To fully embrace failure as a learning opportunity, it is important to cultivate a supportive and encouraging environment. Educational psychologists encourage students to seek feedback from teachers and peers, as constructive criticism can provide valuable insights for growth. By creating a safe space for students to share their failures and learn from them, educational institutions can foster a culture that promotes continuous improvement and resilience.

In conclusion, embracing failure as a learning opportunity is a paradigm shift that can transform the way students approach their education. By reframing failure as an essential part of the learning process, students can develop resilience, a growth mindset, and problem-solving skills. In an environment that encourages learning from failure, students can unlock their full potential and achieve academic and personal success.

Developing Resilience and Perseverance

Resilience and perseverance are two crucial qualities that can greatly impact a student's educational journey and overall success. In this subchapter, we will explore the power of these qualities and provide strategies to develop and strengthen them.

Resilience can be defined as the ability to bounce back from setbacks, challenges, or failures. It is an essential skill that allows students to navigate through the ups and downs of their academic careers. When faced with obstacles, resilient students view them as opportunities for growth rather than insurmountable barriers. They understand that setbacks are temporary and can be overcome with the right mindset and effort.

One strategy to develop resilience is to cultivate a positive mindset. By focusing on the positive aspects of a situation, students can reframe setbacks as learning experiences and find the motivation to keep going. It is important to remember that failure is a natural part of the learning process and should not be seen as a reflection of one's abilities or worth. Embracing a growth mindset, which believes that abilities can be developed through dedication and hard work, can also foster resilience.

Perseverance, on the other hand, is the ability to persist in the face of challenges or difficulties. It is the determination to keep going even when things get tough. Persevering students understand that success often requires sustained effort and are willing to put in the necessary work to achieve their goals.

To develop perseverance, it is important to set realistic and achievable goals. Break down bigger tasks into smaller, manageable steps, and celebrate each milestone achieved along the way. This not only provides a sense of accomplishment but also encourages students to keep moving forward. Additionally, surrounding oneself with a supportive network of peers, mentors, or educators can provide the necessary encouragement and motivation during difficult times.

Ultimately, developing resilience and perseverance is a lifelong journey. It requires self-reflection, self-belief, and a commitment to continuous growth. By embracing challenges, maintaining a positive mindset, and remaining determined in the face of adversity, students can unlock their true potential and achieve academic success.

In conclusion, resilience and perseverance are invaluable qualities that can greatly enhance a student's educational experience. By developing these skills, students can overcome setbacks, embrace challenges, and achieve their goals. Remember, your mindset and attitude have the power to shape your academic journey. With a positive outlook and a determination to persevere, you can unlock your full potential and achieve greatness.

Seeking Support and Building a Supportive Network

In the journey towards achieving academic success, it is crucial for students to recognize the significance of seeking support and building a supportive network. Educational psychology emphasizes the role of social support in promoting student achievement, and this subchapter will delve into the various ways students can harness the power of support to enhance their positive mindset and ultimately excel in their academic pursuits.

One of the first steps in seeking support is recognizing the need for it. Students must understand that they do not have to navigate the challenges of education alone. Whether it is struggling with a difficult subject, feeling overwhelmed by coursework, or facing personal obstacles, seeking support is a proactive approach that can make a significant difference in their educational journey.

There are numerous avenues for seeking support. Students can turn to their teachers, who are not only experts in their respective subjects but also possess valuable insights and resources to assist struggling students. Additionally, classmates can serve as a support network, as they can offer different perspectives, collaborate on assignments, and provide motivation during challenging times.

Outside the classroom, students can also benefit from seeking support from family and friends. These individuals can offer emotional support, encouragement, and a listening ear. Sometimes, simply discussing academic challenges with someone who understands can alleviate stress and help students gain a fresh perspective.

Building a supportive network is equally important. Actively seeking out like-minded individuals who share similar goals and aspirations can create a positive environment that fosters growth and success. Joining study groups, clubs, or organizations that align with students' interests not only provides an opportunity for collaboration but also allows for the development of lasting friendships.

In addition to seeking support from others, it is essential for students to cultivate self-support. Adopting a positive mindset, practicing self-care, and maintaining a healthy work-life balance are crucial aspects of self-support. Students should prioritize their physical and mental well-being, as this directly impacts their ability to learn and perform at their best.

In conclusion, seeking support and building a supportive network are essential strategies for students to cultivate a positive mindset and achieve academic success. Educational psychology highlights the importance of social support in helping students overcome challenges and reach their full potential. By recognizing the need for support, seeking assistance from teachers, classmates, family, and friends, and actively building a supportive network, students can create an environment that fosters growth, motivation, and achievement. Embracing these strategies will empower students to navigate the complexities of education with confidence and resilience.

Chapter 5: Maintaining a Positive Mindset

Practicing Gratitude and Appreciation

In today's fast-paced world, it's easy to get caught up in the whirlwind of academic demands, social pressures, and personal challenges. As students, we often find ourselves overwhelmed and stressed, constantly striving for success while forgetting to appreciate the journey and the small victories along the way. However, cultivating a mindset of gratitude and appreciation can bring about a profound positive transformation in our lives.

Gratitude is the practice of acknowledging and appreciating the good things in our lives, whether big or small. It allows us to shift our focus from what's lacking to what we already have, fostering a sense of contentment and well-being. Research in educational psychology has shown that cultivating gratitude can enhance our mental health, increase our resilience, and improve our overall academic performance.

So, how can we incorporate gratitude and appreciation into our daily lives? It starts with developing a mindfulness practice. Take a few moments each day to reflect on the things you are grateful for. It could be something as simple as a sunny day, a kind word from a friend, or a teacher who went the extra mile to help you. By consciously acknowledging these positive experiences, we train our minds to focus on the good rather than dwelling on the negatives.

Another powerful way to practice gratitude is through acts of kindness. By expressing appreciation to others, we not only make them feel valued but also cultivate a sense of gratitude within ourselves. Write a thank-you note to a teacher who has inspired you, help a classmate with their assignments, or volunteer in your community. These acts of kindness not only make a difference in the lives of others but also remind us of the abundance of goodness around us.

Moreover, keeping a gratitude journal can be an effective tool to develop a positive mindset. Set aside a few minutes each day to write down three things you are grateful for. It could be an achievement, a personal quality, or a positive event. By regularly noting down these moments of gratitude, you create a tangible reminder of the good things in your life, which can be immensely helpful during challenging times.

In conclusion, practicing gratitude and appreciation is a powerful strategy for student achievement. By cultivating a mindset of gratitude, we enhance our mental well-being, increase our resilience, and improve our academic performance. So, let's take a moment to reflect on the good things in our lives, express appreciation to others, and keep a gratitude journal. By doing so, we can transform our mindset and unleash the power of positivity within us.

Mindfulness and Meditation Techniques

In today's fast-paced world, students often find themselves overwhelmed with academic pressures, social challenges, and personal responsibilities. As a result, their mental well-being and academic performance may suffer. This is where mindfulness and meditation techniques come into play. By incorporating these practices into their daily routine, students can develop a positive mindset and achieve greater success in their educational journey.

Mindfulness is the art of being fully present and aware of the current moment, without judgment or attachment. It involves paying attention to one's thoughts, feelings, and physical sensations. By practicing mindfulness, students can enhance their self-awareness and gain control over their emotions. This, in turn, can help them manage stress, improve their focus, and make better decisions.

Meditation, on the other hand, is a practice that involves training the mind to achieve a state of calm and clarity. By engaging in regular meditation sessions, students can develop a greater sense of inner peace and tranquility. This can have a profound impact on their overall mental health and well-being. Additionally, meditation can improve cognitive abilities such as memory, concentration, and creativity, which are vital for educational success.

So, how can students incorporate mindfulness and meditation techniques into their daily lives? Here are some practical strategies:

1. Start with short sessions: Begin by dedicating just a few minutes each day to mindfulness or meditation. Gradually increase the duration as you become more comfortable with the practice.

2. Create a quiet space: Find a peaceful corner in your home or campus where you can meditate without distractions. Make it a comfortable and inviting environment.

3. Focus on your breath: Pay attention to your breath as it goes in and out. This simple act of observing your breath can help anchor your attention to the present moment.

4. Practice gratitude: Take a moment each day to reflect on the things you are grateful for. This can help shift your mindset towards positivity and enhance your overall well-being.

5. Use guided meditation apps: There are numerous smartphone apps available that offer guided meditation sessions. These can be a helpful tool for beginners or those who prefer structure and guidance.

By incorporating mindfulness and meditation techniques into their lives, students can cultivate a positive mindset, reduce stress, and improve their overall well-being. These practices have the potential to transform their educational experience and set them up for greater success in their academic endeavors. So, take a deep breath, find your center, and embark on a journey of self-discovery and personal growth through mindfulness and meditation.

Surrounding Yourself with Positive Influences

In the journey of achieving success as a student, the power of surrounding yourself with positive influences cannot be underestimated. The people and environment that you choose to be a part of greatly impact your mindset, motivation, and ultimately, your academic achievements. This subchapter aims to shed light on the significance of surrounding yourself with positive influences and how it can enhance your educational psychology.

First and foremost, positive influences provide you with a supportive network that encourages personal growth and development. Being surrounded by individuals who believe in your abilities and inspire you to strive for greatness can have a profound impact on your mindset. When you are surrounded by positive influences, you are more likely to adopt their optimistic outlook and overcome obstacles with determination and resilience. Whether it is your friends, family, or mentors, having people who uplift and motivate you can significantly enhance your educational journey.

Moreover, positive influences can broaden your horizons and expose you to new perspectives. Engaging with individuals who have diverse backgrounds, experiences, and knowledge can expand your understanding of various subjects and encourage critical thinking. By surrounding yourself with positive influences, you create an environment that fosters intellectual curiosity and stimulates your desire to learn. This exposure to different ideas and viewpoints can enhance your educational psychology and help you excel academically.

Additionally, positive influences can serve as role models and mentors, guiding you towards success. When you surround yourself with individuals who have achieved great things or possess qualities you admire, you are likely to emulate their positive behaviors and habits. This can include effective time management skills, study techniques, or even a positive mindset. By observing and learning from these positive influences, you can adopt their strategies and incorporate them into your own academic journey.

In conclusion, surrounding yourself with positive influences is a crucial element in fostering a positive mindset and achieving student success. The people you choose to surround yourself with can greatly impact your motivation, mindset, and overall educational psychology. By surrounding yourself with individuals who believe in your abilities, expose you to new perspectives, and serve as role models, you create an environment that encourages personal growth and academic achievement. So, be mindful of the influences you allow into your life and strive to surround yourself with positivity as you navigate the path towards success as a student.

Chapter 6: Strategies for Effective Studying

Creating a Productive Study Environment

In the pursuit of academic success, one of the most crucial factors that students often overlook is creating a productive study environment. The environment in which you study plays a significant role in your ability to focus, retain information, and ultimately achieve your educational goals. This subchapter will guide you through the essential strategies and techniques to help you cultivate an optimal study environment that maximizes your learning potential.

First and foremost, it is vital to find a quiet and distraction-free space to study. Eliminate any external noises or interruptions that can hinder your concentration. Turn off your phone or put it on silent mode to avoid being tempted by social media notifications or text messages. Consider using noise-canceling headphones or ambient background music to create a serene atmosphere conducive to learning.

Another crucial aspect of a productive study environment is ensuring that your study area is well-organized and clutter-free. A tidy and organized space can enhance your focus and prevent unnecessary distractions. Keep all your study materials, such as textbooks, notebooks, and stationery, within reach. Utilize storage solutions like shelves, drawers, or desk organizers to maintain order and efficiency in your study space.

Lighting is another essential element to consider when creating an optimal study environment. Natural light is ideal, as it promotes alertness and reduces eye strain. If natural light is limited, invest in a good desk lamp that provides sufficient illumination without causing glare on your study materials.

Comfort is also crucial for maintaining productivity during long study sessions. Ensure that your study area is ergonomically designed, with a comfortable chair and a suitable desk height. Take regular breaks to stretch and move around to prevent fatigue and increase blood circulation.

Lastly, personalize your study environment to make it more inspiring and motivating. Surround yourself with visual cues that remind you of your goals and aspirations. Hang up motivational quotes, images, or even a vision board to keep you focused and driven. Consider incorporating plants or other elements of nature into your study space, as research suggests that exposure to nature can boost cognitive function and overall well-being.

Remember, creating a productive study environment is a personal journey. Experiment with different strategies and techniques to discover what works best for you. By implementing these practices, you will be setting yourself up for success and unlocking your full potential in the educational realm.

In conclusion, a productive study environment is the foundation for academic achievement. By finding a quiet and distraction-free space, keeping your study area organized, optimizing lighting and comfort, and personalizing your surroundings, you will be able to maximize your learning potential. Embrace the power of a positive mindset and take control of your study environment to pave the way for your success in educational psychology.

Time Management and Prioritization

Time Management and Prioritization: Achieving Success through Effective Planning

In the fast-paced and demanding world of education, students often find themselves overwhelmed with multiple tasks, deadlines, and commitments. The ability to manage time efficiently and prioritize tasks is crucial to achieving academic success and maintaining a positive mindset. This subchapter will delve into the strategies and techniques of time management and prioritization, empowering students to take control of their schedules and achieve their goals.

Understanding the importance of time management is the first step towards effective planning. Time is a finite resource, and it is essential to allocate it wisely. By creating a schedule or using a planner, students can visualize their commitments and responsibilities, ensuring that no task is overlooked or neglected. Breaking down larger tasks into smaller, manageable ones is another effective strategy, allowing students to tackle them systematically and avoid feeling overwhelmed.

Prioritization is the key to organizing one's time effectively. By identifying and categorizing tasks based on urgency and importance, students can allocate their time and effort accordingly. The Eisenhower Matrix, a popular time management tool, can aid students in distinguishing between urgent tasks that require immediate attention and important tasks that contribute to long-term goals. This matrix helps students prioritize tasks and avoid wasting time on trivial matters that do not contribute to their overall success.

Additionally, students should consider their personal energy levels and work habits when planning their time. Understanding when they are most productive allows students to schedule their most challenging tasks during their peak performance periods. This approach ensures that important tasks receive the attention and focus they require, increasing efficiency and productivity.

Time management and prioritization also involve eliminating procrastination, a common challenge faced by many students. Procrastination often leads to increased stress, decreased productivity, and missed deadlines. Techniques such as the Pomodoro Technique, which involves working in focused bursts followed by short breaks, can help students overcome procrastination and maintain focus on their tasks.

In conclusion, mastering time management and prioritization is essential for students to achieve their academic goals and maintain a positive mindset. By effectively planning their time, identifying priorities, and eliminating procrastination, students can take control of their schedules and achieve success. This subchapter provides students with the tools and strategies necessary to manage their time efficiently, fostering a positive and productive educational journey. With a positive mindset and effective time management, students can unlock their full potential and thrive in their educational endeavors.

Active Learning Techniques

In the pursuit of academic success, it is crucial for students to adopt effective learning strategies that go beyond passive listening and memorization. This subchapter explores the concept of active learning techniques, which have been proven to enhance student engagement, critical thinking, and overall academic achievement. By actively participating in the learning process, students can develop a deeper understanding of the subject matter and apply their knowledge in practical ways.

One of the most effective active learning techniques is classroom discussion. Engaging in meaningful conversations with classmates and instructors allows students to share ideas, challenge assumptions, and develop a broader perspective on the subject matter. Through active participation in discussions, students can refine their communication skills, improve their ability to articulate thoughts, and gain valuable insights from diverse viewpoints.

Another powerful technique is problem-solving. Rather than simply absorbing information, students are encouraged to apply what they have learned to real-life scenarios. This hands-on approach not only strengthens understanding but also hones critical thinking skills. By actively seeking solutions to problems, students develop their analytical abilities, creativity, and decision-making skills.

Collaborative learning is yet another effective technique that fosters active engagement. Working in groups or pairs allows students to exchange knowledge, brainstorm ideas, and learn from one another. Through collaboration, students gain a deeper appreciation for teamwork, improve their social skills, and expand their understanding through exposure to different perspectives.

Active learning can also be facilitated through the use of technology. Online forums, interactive quizzes, and multimedia content enable students to actively participate in the learning process beyond traditional classroom settings. These tools provide opportunities for self-assessment, immediate feedback, and personalized learning experiences, ensuring that students remain actively engaged in their educational journey.

In conclusion, active learning techniques are powerful tools that can significantly enhance student achievement. By fostering engagement, critical thinking, and collaboration, students are better equipped to absorb, retain, and apply knowledge. Whether through classroom discussions, problem-solving activities, group work, or the integration of technology, active learning techniques empower students to become active participants in their own education. By adopting these strategies, students can unlock their true potential and develop a positive mindset towards learning, setting themselves up for lifelong success.

Chapter 7: Overcoming Procrastination

Understanding the Causes of Procrastination

Procrastination is a common problem faced by students across the globe. It is a habit that can hinder academic success and personal growth. In order to overcome procrastination, it is essential to understand its causes and address them effectively. This subchapter aims to shed light on the underlying reasons behind procrastination, providing valuable insights into the field of educational psychology.

One of the main causes of procrastination is poor time management skills. Students often struggle to prioritize their tasks effectively and allocate appropriate time for each activity. This leads to a build-up of unfinished tasks, causing stress and anxiety. By understanding the importance of time management and incorporating strategies like creating a schedule, setting deadlines, and breaking tasks into smaller, manageable parts, students can overcome this hurdle and become more productive.

Another cause of procrastination is fear of failure. Students may delay starting a task due to the fear of not achieving the desired outcome. This fear can be paralyzing and prevent students from even trying. Educational psychology teaches us that developing a growth mindset, wherein failures are seen as opportunities for learning and growth, can help overcome this fear. By reframing failure as a stepping stone to success, students can find the motivation to start and complete their tasks.

Moreover, perfectionism can also contribute to procrastination. Students who have high expectations of themselves may delay starting a task if they feel they cannot meet their own standards. This can lead to a never-ending cycle of delay and disappointment. Educational psychology suggests that adopting a more realistic and flexible approach, focusing on progress rather than perfection, can help students overcome perfectionism and boost their productivity.

Lastly, lack of motivation is a significant cause of procrastination. Students may struggle to find intrinsic motivation for certain tasks, making it challenging to start or complete them. By understanding the importance of setting goals, finding personal reasons for completing a task, and incorporating rewards and incentives, students can enhance their motivation levels and conquer procrastination.

In conclusion, understanding the causes of procrastination is crucial for students seeking to overcome this habit. By delving into the field of educational psychology, students can gain valuable insights into the underlying factors contributing to procrastination. By addressing poor time management skills, fear of failure, perfectionism, and lack of motivation, students can develop a positive mindset and achieve greater success in their academic pursuits.

Breaking Tasks into Manageable Steps

In the journey towards academic success, students often face numerous challenges and overwhelming tasks. Whether it's writing a research paper, studying for exams, or completing a long-term project, the sheer magnitude of these tasks can leave students feeling stressed and discouraged. However, by adopting the strategy of breaking tasks into manageable steps, students can overcome these obstacles and achieve their goals with a positive mindset.

Breaking tasks into manageable steps is an effective approach rooted in educational psychology that helps students maintain focus, manage time efficiently, and reduce anxiety. By dividing a larger task into smaller, more manageable sub-tasks, students can approach their work in a systematic and organized manner. This approach not only makes the task appear less daunting but also increases the likelihood of success.

Firstly, breaking tasks into manageable steps allows students to maintain focus and avoid feeling overwhelmed. When faced with a complex project, students may find it difficult to even begin. However, by creating a step-by-step plan, students can start with the first sub-task and gradually progress towards the next. This helps in maintaining concentration and prevents distractions, as students are able to focus solely on the immediate step at hand.

Secondly, this approach enables students to manage their time efficiently. By breaking a larger task into smaller steps, students can allocate realistic time frames for each sub-task. This helps in creating a structured study schedule, allowing students to devote adequate time to each step without feeling rushed. Furthermore, completing smaller tasks within a specified timeframe boosts motivation and provides a sense of accomplishment, encouraging students to continue making progress.

Lastly, breaking tasks into manageable steps helps reduce anxiety and increases self-confidence. When faced with a seemingly insurmountable challenge, students often feel overwhelmed, leading to heightened stress levels. However, by dividing the task into smaller, more achievable steps, students can approach each sub-task with greater ease and confidence. As they successfully complete each step, their self-belief and motivation grow, reinforcing a positive mindset that carries them through the entire project.

In conclusion, breaking tasks into manageable steps is a powerful strategy rooted in educational psychology that can benefit students in achieving their academic goals. By adopting this approach, students can maintain focus, manage time effectively, and reduce anxiety, ultimately leading to increased productivity and success. So, the next time you encounter a challenging task, remember to break it down into smaller, more manageable steps and watch how your positive mindset propels you towards achievement.

Utilizing Procrastination-Busting Techniques

Procrastination is a common issue that many students face, causing unnecessary stress and hindering academic success. However, with the right mindset and some effective techniques, you can overcome procrastination and achieve your goals. In this subchapter, we will explore various strategies to help you bust through procrastination and develop a positive mindset towards your studies.

One powerful technique is the "5-Minute Rule." This rule suggests that you commit to working on a task for just five minutes. Often, the hardest part is getting started, so by setting a short time frame, you remove the pressure of doing it all at once. Once those five minutes are up, you'll likely find yourself more engaged and motivated to continue.

Another effective technique is to break your tasks into smaller, more manageable chunks. When faced with a daunting assignment, it's easy to become overwhelmed and put it off. By breaking it down into smaller parts, you can tackle one step at a time, making the task seem less daunting and more achievable.

Creating a schedule or to-do list is also essential. Prioritize your tasks based on urgency and importance, and allocate specific time slots for each task. By having a clear plan, you'll be less likely to procrastinate and more likely to stay focused and productive.

Accountability can be a powerful motivator. Consider finding a study buddy or joining a study group where you can hold each other accountable for completing tasks and staying on track. Sharing your goals and progress with others can provide the necessary push to overcome procrastination and achieve your desired outcomes.

Additionally, understanding your personal procrastination triggers is crucial. Is it social media? Fear of failure? Lack of interest? Identifying these triggers will allow you to develop strategies to combat them. For instance, you could use website blockers to limit access to distracting websites, establish a reward system to motivate yourself, or find ways to make the task more engaging or relevant to your interests.

Finally, embracing a positive mindset is key to overcoming procrastination. Focus on the benefits of completing tasks promptly, such as reduced stress and more free time. Celebrate your small victories along the way, and remind yourself of your long-term goals and aspirations. By adopting a positive mindset, you can reframe procrastination as an opportunity for growth and self-improvement.

In conclusion, procrastination can be conquered with the right mindset and effective techniques. By implementing strategies such as the 5-Minute Rule, task breakdown, scheduling, accountability, understanding triggers, and embracing a positive mindset, you can bust through procrastination and achieve academic success. Remember, your mindset is a powerful tool, and with determination and perseverance, you can overcome any obstacle on your path to success.

Chapter 8: Building Confidence in Academic Performance

Effective Test Preparation Strategies

In the fast-paced world of academics, students often find themselves overwhelmed with exams and assessments. This subchapter aims to equip students with effective test preparation strategies that will not only enhance their performance but also foster a positive mindset towards their studies. By incorporating these strategies into their study routine, students can achieve higher levels of success and overcome the challenges associated with test anxiety.

One of the most vital steps in effective test preparation is creating a study schedule. By organizing study sessions in advance, students can allocate sufficient time to cover all the necessary material without feeling rushed or overwhelmed. Breaking down the study material into smaller, manageable chunks and dedicating specific time slots to each topic ensures comprehensive learning and retention.

Another essential strategy is active learning. Instead of passively reading through textbooks or lecture notes, students should engage in active learning techniques such as summarizing information in their own words, creating flashcards, or teaching the material to a friend. These techniques promote better understanding and retention of the subject matter.

Practice tests play a crucial role in effective test preparation as well. By simulating exam-like conditions, students can familiarize themselves with the format and types of questions they are likely to encounter. Regularly taking practice tests not only helps students identify their strengths and weaknesses but also builds their confidence and reduces test anxiety.

Furthermore, it is essential for students to adopt effective time management strategies during exams. By carefully allocating time to each question or section, students can ensure that they complete the exam within the given time frame. Prioritizing questions and tackling the easier ones first can also help in maximizing scores and reducing stress.

Lastly, adopting a positive mindset is crucial for success in test preparation. Students should focus on their strengths rather than dwelling on their weaknesses. Cultivating a growth mindset, where challenges are viewed as opportunities for growth, can significantly impact academic performance. Positive self-talk, visualization techniques, and relaxation exercises can also help alleviate test anxiety and enhance overall performance.

In conclusion, effective test preparation strategies are instrumental in achieving academic success. By implementing a well-organized study schedule, engaging in active learning techniques, practicing with mock tests, managing time efficiently, and maintaining a positive mindset, students can overcome test anxiety and perform at their best. These strategies, rooted in educational psychology principles, empower students to approach exams with confidence, resilience, and a growth mindset.

Managing Test Anxiety

Test anxiety is a common experience that many students face when it comes to taking exams. This overwhelming feeling of stress and unease can negatively impact performance and hinder academic success. However, with the right strategies and a positive mindset, it is possible to manage and overcome test anxiety, allowing students to perform at their best.

1. Preparation is key: One of the most effective ways to combat test anxiety is through thorough preparation. Start by creating a study schedule well in advance of the exam, allowing ample time for review. Break down the material into smaller, manageable chunks, and use various study techniques such as flashcards, summarizing key points, or teaching the material to someone else. By being well-prepared, you will feel more confident and less anxious about the upcoming test.

2. Adopt a positive mindset: Your mindset plays a significant role in how you approach and handle test anxiety. Instead of viewing exams as threats, reframe them as opportunities to showcase your knowledge and skills. Believe in your abilities and focus on your strengths. Replace negative self-talk with positive affirmations such as "I am prepared and capable of doing well on this test." Visualization techniques can also be helpful in visualizing success and reducing anxiety.

3. Practice relaxation techniques: When test anxiety strikes, it is important to have relaxation techniques in your toolkit. Deep breathing exercises, progressive muscle relaxation, and meditation can help calm your mind and body. Practice these techniques regularly, not just during exams, to build resilience and manage stress in other areas of your life as well.

4. Create a supportive environment: Surround yourself with a supportive network of friends, family, and mentors who can provide encouragement and reassurance during times of anxiety. Share your concerns and seek their guidance. Additionally, consider forming study groups or seeking extra help from teachers or tutors. Collaborating with others can help alleviate anxiety and provide different perspectives on the material.

5. Take care of yourself: Prioritize self-care to maintain a healthy body and mind. Get enough sleep, eat well-balanced meals, and engage in regular physical activity. Avoid excessive caffeine or energy drinks before exams, as they can increase anxiety levels. Remember to take breaks during study sessions to rest and recharge.

By implementing these strategies and adopting a positive mindset, you can effectively manage test anxiety and perform at your best. Remember, exams are just one measure of your abilities, and your worth as a student goes beyond test scores. Believe in yourself, stay focused, and strive for progress rather than perfection. With the power of a positive mindset, you can conquer test anxiety and achieve academic success.

Developing Effective Study Habits

In today's fast-paced world, where distractions are everywhere, developing effective study habits is more important than ever. As students, it is crucial to understand the power of a positive mindset and implement strategies that will help us achieve academic success. This subchapter will delve into the realm of developing effective study habits, providing valuable insights and techniques to enhance our learning experience.

One of the first steps in developing effective study habits is to create a conducive environment for learning. Find a quiet and comfortable space where you can focus without distractions. Eliminate any potential interruptions, such as turning off your phone or closing unnecessary tabs on your computer. By creating a designated study area, you are mentally preparing yourself to engage in productive learning.

Another key aspect of effective study habits is time management. Plan your study sessions in advance, allocating specific time slots for each subject or task. Break down your study material into manageable chunks, allowing for regular breaks to avoid burnout. By adhering to a structured study schedule, you can optimize your learning potential and retain information more effectively.

Additionally, it is crucial to adopt active learning strategies. Instead of passively reading or highlighting textbooks, engage in activities that promote active understanding and retention. This can include summarizing information in your own words, creating flashcards, or teaching the material to a friend or family member. By actively participating in the learning process, you are more likely to remember and comprehend the information.

Furthermore, developing effective study habits involves recognizing and leveraging your unique learning style. Some individuals are visual learners, while others are auditory or kinesthetic learners. Experiment with different study techniques to identify which methods work best for you. Utilize visual aids, listen to recorded lectures, or incorporate hands-on activities to cater to your specific learning style.

Lastly, maintain a positive mindset throughout your academic journey. Believing in your ability to succeed and adopting a growth mindset will enhance your motivation and resilience. Embrace challenges as opportunities for growth, and celebrate your achievements along the way. By cultivating a positive mindset, you will overcome obstacles and reach your full potential.

In conclusion, developing effective study habits is essential for students seeking academic success. By creating a conducive environment, managing your time effectively, adopting active learning strategies, recognizing your learning style, and maintaining a positive mindset, you can optimize your learning potential and achieve your goals. Embrace the power of a positive mindset and unleash your true potential.

Chapter 9: Goal Setting and Achievement

Setting SMART Goals

In the journey of student achievement, one powerful tool that can propel you towards success is setting SMART goals. Whether you are striving for academic excellence, personal growth, or career advancement, having clear and well-defined objectives is essential. This subchapter will guide you through the process of setting and achieving SMART goals, using proven strategies from the field of educational psychology.

SMART is an acronym that stands for Specific, Measurable, Achievable, Relevant, and Time-bound. Let's delve deeper into each component:

Specific: A goal should be precise and well-defined. Instead of saying, "I want to improve my grades," try articulating, "I aim to raise my math grade from a B- to an A by the end of the semester." Being specific allows you to focus your efforts and create a clear path towards success.

Measurable: It is crucial to track your progress and determine whether you are moving in the right direction. Establishing measurable criteria helps you stay accountable and motivated. For instance, you can measure your progress by setting milestones and tracking the number of hours you dedicate to studying each week.

Achievable: While goals should challenge you, they should also be within your reach. Setting unattainable goals can lead to frustration and demotivation. Consider your abilities, resources, and constraints to ensure that your goals are realistic and achievable.

Relevant: Goals should align with your long-term aspirations and values. Ask yourself, "Why is this goal important to me?" Make sure your goals are meaningful and contribute to your overall growth and success.

Time-bound: Setting a deadline helps create a sense of urgency and prevents procrastination. It also allows you to break down your goals into smaller, manageable tasks. For example, if your goal is to finish reading a book, set a deadline of one week and divide the reading into daily chunks.

By setting SMART goals, you become an active participant in your own success. These goals provide clarity, direction, and motivation as you navigate through your educational journey. Remember to review and revise your goals periodically to ensure they remain relevant and attainable.

In conclusion, the power of setting SMART goals cannot be underestimated. As students, utilizing the strategies of educational psychology can significantly enhance your achievement. Embrace the practice of setting Specific, Measurable, Achievable, Relevant, and Time-bound goals, and witness the transformative impact it has on your academic and personal growth.

Tracking Progress and Celebrating Milestones

In the journey towards achieving our goals, it is essential to track our progress and celebrate milestones along the way. This subchapter will delve into the importance of monitoring our advancement and the positive impact it can have on our motivation and overall achievement. By understanding the principles of educational psychology, we can harness the power of a positive mindset to propel ourselves forward.

Tracking progress is instrumental in maintaining focus and motivation. When we have a clear idea of how far we have come, it becomes easier to stay driven and continue working towards our objectives. By setting specific and measurable goals, we can break our big aspirations into smaller, manageable tasks. Regularly checking off these smaller milestones provides a sense of accomplishment and boosts our confidence. It reinforces the notion that we are making progress, no matter how small, and encourages us to keep going.

Educational psychology teaches us that feedback is crucial for growth. By tracking our progress, we can objectively assess our performance and identify areas that need improvement. This self-reflection allows us to make necessary adjustments, refine our strategies, and enhance our learning experience. It also helps us identify patterns and trends, allowing us to recognize what works best for us and what doesn't. This self-awareness is a powerful tool that can guide us towards more effective approaches and ultimately lead to greater success.

Celebrating milestones is equally significant in maintaining motivation and fostering a positive mindset. Each milestone reached is a cause for celebration, no matter how big or small. By acknowledging our achievements, we reinforce a positive cycle of accomplishment and reward. This positive reinforcement strengthens our belief in our abilities and encourages us to persevere through challenges.

Moreover, celebrating milestones provides an opportunity for reflection and gratitude. It allows us to appreciate the effort, dedication, and resilience we have demonstrated throughout our journey. By expressing gratitude towards ourselves and others who have supported us, we cultivate a positive mindset that further fuels our motivation and propels us towards future achievements.

In conclusion, tracking progress and celebrating milestones are essential components in the pursuit of student achievement. By applying principles from educational psychology and embracing a positive mindset, we can harness these strategies to stay motivated, assess our performance, make necessary adjustments, and ultimately celebrate our successes. Let us embrace the power of progress tracking and milestone celebrations as vital tools on our path to accomplishing our goals.

Overcoming Challenges and Staying Motivated

In the journey of student achievement, challenges and obstacles are inevitable. However, it is the ability to overcome these hurdles and maintain motivation that separates successful students from the rest. This subchapter aims to provide valuable insights and strategies to help students overcome challenges and stay motivated throughout their educational journey.

One of the first steps towards overcoming challenges is to develop a positive mindset. Educational psychology emphasizes the power of positive thinking, as it can significantly impact your ability to overcome obstacles. By cultivating a positive mindset, you can approach challenges as opportunities for growth and learning, rather than as roadblocks. Recognize that setbacks are a natural part of the learning process, and view them as valuable learning experiences rather than failures.

Another key aspect of overcoming challenges is setting realistic goals. It is essential to have a clear vision of what you want to achieve and break it down into smaller, manageable goals. By setting realistic goals, you can maintain a sense of progress and accomplishment, which in turn fuels motivation. Celebrate each milestone you achieve, no matter how small, as it will reinforce your determination and drive.

Furthermore, it is crucial to seek support and build a network of like-minded individuals. Surround yourself with people who believe in your abilities and can provide guidance and encouragement during challenging times. Collaborating with peers and forming study groups can also be beneficial, as you can share knowledge, resources, and support each other through difficult assignments or exams.

When facing difficulties, it is essential to adopt a problem-solving approach rather than dwelling on the problem itself. Break down the challenge into smaller, more manageable tasks, and develop a plan to tackle them one at a time. This approach helps maintain focus and prevents overwhelming feelings that may demotivate you.

Lastly, staying motivated requires maintaining a healthy work-life balance. It is crucial to take breaks, rest, and engage in activities that bring you joy and relaxation. Recognize that your mental and physical well-being are essential for optimal academic performance. By taking care of yourself, you can stay motivated and overcome challenges more effectively.

In conclusion, overcoming challenges and staying motivated is crucial for student achievement. By developing a positive mindset, setting realistic goals, seeking support, adopting a problem-solving approach, and maintaining a healthy work-life balance, students can navigate through obstacles and maintain their motivation. Remember, challenges are opportunities for growth, and with the right mindset and strategies, you can overcome any hurdle that comes your way.

Chapter 10: Creating a Positive Learning Environment

Developing Positive Relationships with Teachers and Peers

Having positive relationships with both your teachers and peers is crucial for your academic success and personal growth. In this subchapter, we will explore the importance of building these relationships and provide you with practical strategies to cultivate positive connections in your educational journey.

Teachers play a vital role in your education. They are not only responsible for imparting knowledge but can also serve as mentors, guides, and sources of inspiration. Developing a positive relationship with your teachers can greatly enhance your learning experience. Start by showing respect and gratitude towards them. Participate actively in class, ask questions, and offer your insights. This will not only demonstrate your dedication but also show your teachers that you value their expertise.

Building rapport with your teachers involves effective communication. Be open and honest with them about your strengths, weaknesses, and academic goals. Seek their advice and guidance whenever needed. Remember, teachers are there to support you, and by involving them in your learning process, you can create a nurturing environment that fosters growth and achievement.

Equally important are the relationships you build with your peers. Peer relationships can provide a sense of belonging, collaboration opportunities, and emotional support. Surround yourself with positive-minded peers who share your academic goals and motivate you to excel. Engage in group study sessions, form study groups, and participate in extracurricular activities together. These interactions can help you learn from one another, develop new perspectives, and enhance your problem-solving skills.

Respecting your peers is essential in maintaining positive relationships. Treat them with kindness, empathy, and understanding. Avoid gossip or negative behavior that can create a toxic environment. Instead, be supportive and celebrate each other's achievements. By creating a supportive community, you will find that your academic journey becomes more enjoyable and fulfilling.

In conclusion, developing positive relationships with teachers and peers is essential for your educational and personal growth. By showing respect, gratitude, and effective communication with your teachers, you can create a nurturing learning environment. Similarly, building supportive relationships with your peers fosters collaboration, emotional support, and a sense of belonging. Remember, the power of positive mindset extends beyond individual achievements; it also lies in cultivating a positive community that supports and uplifts one another.

Active Participation and Engagement in Class

One of the key factors that contribute to student achievement is active participation and engagement in the classroom. In order to succeed academically, students must go beyond simply attending classes and listening to lectures. They must actively participate in their own learning process and engage with the material being presented. This subchapter aims to provide students with motivational strategies to foster active participation and engagement in class.

First and foremost, it is crucial for students to develop a positive mindset towards their education. By embracing a growth mindset, students can believe in their ability to learn and improve. This mindset encourages them to actively participate in class discussions, ask questions, and contribute to group activities. Engaging with the material in this way not only deepens their understanding but also enhances their overall learning experience.

To further enhance engagement, students should take ownership of their learning journey. This involves setting specific goals for each class and actively working towards them. By setting goals, students become more motivated to participate and engage, as they have a clear vision of what they want to achieve. Additionally, students should take responsibility for their own learning by seeking additional resources, participating in study groups, and utilizing available support services.

Another effective strategy to promote active participation is to develop effective study habits. This includes active listening, note-taking, and reviewing the material regularly. Actively listening in class allows students to stay focused and grasp the key concepts being taught. Taking detailed notes helps reinforce their understanding and serves as a valuable resource for future reference. Regularly reviewing the material helps students consolidate their knowledge and identify areas where they may need to seek further clarification.

Moreover, active participation extends beyond the classroom walls. Students should actively engage in extracurricular activities, such as clubs, organizations, and volunteer work. These activities not only provide opportunities for personal growth and skill development but also foster a sense of belonging and community. By actively participating in these activities, students gain a broader perspective and develop valuable interpersonal skills.

In conclusion, active participation and engagement in class are vital for student achievement. By adopting a growth mindset, setting goals, taking ownership of their learning, developing effective study habits, and engaging in extracurricular activities, students can enhance their overall educational experience. By actively participating and engaging in class, students not only improve their academic performance but also develop important life skills that will serve them beyond the classroom.

Embracing a Growth Mindset in Learning

In the journey of academic success, one of the most powerful tools that students can possess is a growth mindset. The concept of a growth mindset, as popularized by renowned psychologist Carol Dweck, is the belief that intelligence and abilities can be developed through dedication, effort, and persistence. It is a mindset that sees challenges as opportunities for growth, setbacks as stepping stones to success, and criticism as a chance to learn and improve.

As students, it is crucial to understand the importance of embracing a growth mindset in our learning endeavors. By adopting this mindset, we can overcome obstacles, increase our motivation, and unlock our true potential. Educational psychology research consistently supports the idea that a growth mindset leads to higher achievement and overall well-being.

First and foremost, embracing a growth mindset allows us to view challenges as opportunities rather than obstacles. Instead of being discouraged by difficult tasks, we approach them with a sense of curiosity and determination. We understand that our abilities can be developed through practice and effort, and thus, we are willing to put in the necessary work to overcome challenges. This mindset empowers us to persevere, even when faced with setbacks or failures, as we believe that these experiences are essential for growth.

Furthermore, a growth mindset fuels our motivation to learn. When we believe that our efforts can lead to improvement, we become more engaged and dedicated to our studies. We are not afraid to take risks or step out of our comfort zones, as we understand that it is through these experiences that we can expand our knowledge and skills. This increased motivation drives us to seek out new opportunities for learning, ask questions, and actively participate in the educational process.

Lastly, embracing a growth mindset allows us to embrace feedback and criticism constructively. Rather than being discouraged by negative feedback, we see it as an opportunity to learn and improve. We understand that feedback provides valuable insights into our strengths and areas for growth. By embracing feedback, we can identify areas that need improvement and develop effective strategies to enhance our learning outcomes.

In conclusion, adopting a growth mindset is crucial for students' success in their educational journey. By embracing this mindset, we can approach challenges with resilience, increase our motivation to learn, and utilize feedback constructively. As students, we have the power to shape our mindset and unlock our true potential for academic achievement and personal growth.

Conclusion: Embracing the Power of a Positive Mindset for Lifelong Success

In this book, "The Power of Positive Mindset: Motivational Strategies for Student Achievement," we have explored the profound impact that a positive mindset can have on student success. Through the lens of educational psychology, we have delved into the various ways in which our mindset shapes our attitudes, behaviors, and ultimately, our achievements.

As students, it is crucial for us to recognize the immense power that lies within our minds. Our mindset can either propel us towards greatness or hold us back from reaching our full potential. By embracing a positive mindset, we can cultivate the mental strength necessary to overcome obstacles, learn from failures, and persist in the face of challenges.

One of the key takeaways from this book is the importance of self-belief. It is essential for us to foster a belief in our own abilities and potential. When we have confidence in ourselves, we are more likely to set ambitious goals and work diligently to achieve them. A positive mindset allows us to view setbacks as opportunities for growth rather than insurmountable roadblocks. By reframing our thinking and focusing on solutions rather than problems, we can develop resilience and tenacity.

Moreover, a positive mindset fosters a love for learning. By approaching our studies with curiosity and enthusiasm, we can unlock the joy of acquiring knowledge. When we embrace a growth mindset, we understand that intelligence and abilities can be developed through effort and dedication. This empowers us to seek out challenges, seek help when needed, and continually strive for improvement.

The power of a positive mindset extends beyond our academic pursuits. It influences our relationships, our well-being, and our overall happiness. By cultivating positive thoughts and attitudes, we can create a supportive and uplifting environment for ourselves and those around us. We become more resilient in the face of adversity, leading to greater overall life satisfaction.

In conclusion, embracing the power of a positive mindset is essential for lifelong success. As students, we must recognize that our mindset is not fixed, but rather a malleable tool that we can shape to our advantage. By adopting a positive mindset, we can overcome challenges, achieve our goals, and ultimately lead fulfilling and successful lives. Let this book serve as a guide to harnessing the power of a positive mindset and unlocking your full potential.